DATE DUE

15195

977.2   Thompson, Kathleen.
Tho
         Indiana

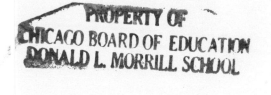

STECK-VAUGHN
PORTRAIT OF AMERICA

Indiana

Steck-Vaughn Company

Executive Editor	Diane Sharpe
Senior Editor	Martin S. Saiewitz
Design Manager	Pamela Heaney
Photo Editor	Margie Foster

Proof Positive/Farrowlyne Associates, Inc.
Program Editorial, Revision Development, Design, and Production

Consultant: Indianapolis Chamber of Commerce

Published by Raintree Steck-Vaughn Publishers, an imprint of Steck-Vaughn Company.

A Turner Educational Services, Inc. book. Based on the Portrait of America television series by R. E. (Ted) Turner.

Cover Photo: Cataract Falls by © SuperStock.

Library of Congress Cataloging-in-Publication Data

Thompson, Kathleen.
   Indiana / Kathleen Thompson.
     p.   cm. — (Portrait of America)
   "A Turner book."
   "Based on the Portrait of America television series"—T.p. verso.
   Includes index.
   ISBN 0-8114-7334-1 (library binding).—ISBN 0-8114-7439-9 (softcover)
   1. Indiana—Juvenile literature. [1. Indiana.] I. Title.
   II. Series: Thompson, Kathleen. Portrait of America.
   F526.3.T46 1996
   977.2—dc20   95-40009
                                          CIP
                                          AC

Printed and Bound in the United States of America

1 2 3 4 5 6 7 8 9 10 WZ 98 97 96 95

Acknowledgments
The publishers wish to thank the following for permission to reproduce photographs:
P. 7 Indiana Department of Tourism; pp. 8, 10 North Wind Picture Archives; p. 11 (top) Photograph by Mall/Indiana Historical Society Library, (bottom) © Ron Woods/Tippecanoe County Historical Association; p. 12 © Richard D. Hawthorne; p. 14 Photograph by Bass Photo Company Collection/Indiana Historical Society Library; p. 15 (top left, top right) Levi Coffin House Association, (bottom) Cook Collection, The Valentine Museum; p. 16 Amaco; p. 17 Studebaker National Museum; p. 18 Elwood Haynes Museum; p. 19 Indiana Department of Tourism; pp. 20, 21 Historic New Harmony; p. 22 U.S. Steel Corporation; p. 24 © Frank A. Cezus/Indiana Port Commission; p. 25 Delco Electronics Inc.; p. 26 © Richard D. Hawthorne; p. 27 (top) Indiana Coal Council, Inc., (bottom) © Richard D. Hawthorne; p. 28 © Steve Swope/Indy 500 Photos; pp. 29, 30 © Indy 500 Photos; p. 31 © Linda McQueeney/Indy 500 Photos; p. 32 © Mark Wick/Indiana High School Athletic Association; p. 34 (top) Indiana University/Instructional Support Services, (bottom) © Alan Singer/CBS; p. 35 © Richard D. Hawthorne; p. 36 (top) Indiana Department of Tourism, (bottom) The Children's Museum of Indianapolis; p. 37 Lincoln National Boyhood Memorial/National Park Service; p. 38 Indiana Department of Tourism; p. 39 © Balthazar Korab; pp. 40, 41 (both) The Shrine to Music Museum/University of South Dakota; p. 42 © Uniphoto; p. 44 © Richard D. Hawthorne; p. 46 One Mile Up; p. 47 (left) One Mile Up, (center) Indiana Department of Tourism, (right) © Photo Researchers.

STECK-VAUGHN

PORTRAIT OF AMERICA

Indiana

Kathleen Thompson

A Turner Book

RSVP

RAINTREE
STECK-VAUGHN
PUBLISHERS

The Steck-Vaughn Company

Austin, Texas

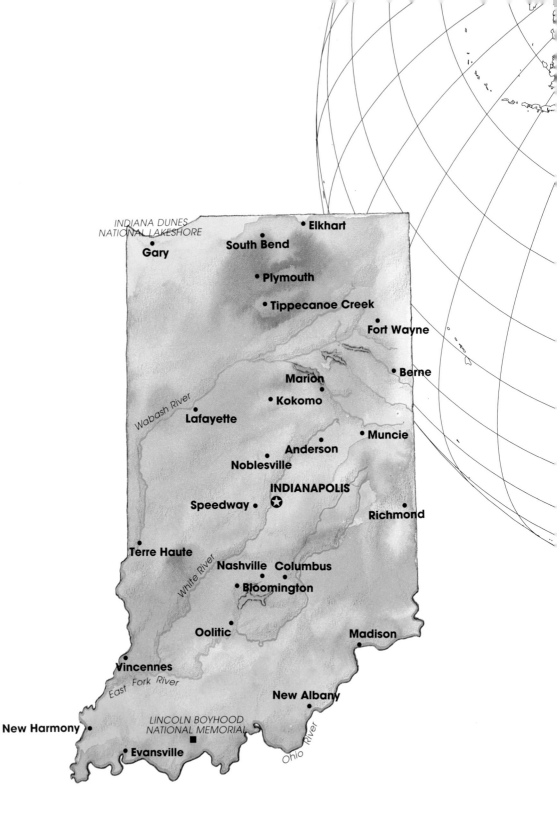

Indiana

INDIANA DUNES
NATIONAL LAKESHORE

Gary

Elkhart

South Bend

Plymouth

Tippecanoe Creek

Fort Wayne

Berne

Marion

Kokomo

Lafayette

Wabash River

Muncie

Anderson

Noblesville

INDIANAPOLIS

Speedway

Richmond

Terre Haute

White River

Nashville   Columbus

Bloomington

Oolitic

Madison

Vincennes

East Fork River

New Albany

New Harmony

LINCOLN BOYHOOD
NATIONAL MEMORIAL

Ohio River

Evansville

Contents

Introduction

Indiana is known as the Crossroads of America. During the late 1800s, many pioneers moving westward passed through some part of this midwestern state. Today, however, Indiana is a destination all its own. It's easy to see why. There's someplace there for everyone. Southern Indiana is a land of forested hills and valleys. The lakes and rolling sand dunes in northern Indiana provide sport and quiet pleasures. The central plains are packed with acres of corn. Where do you want the Crossroads of America to take you?

Indiana Dunes National Lakeshore is a mixture of ancient and recent natural history. The back dunes are thousands of years old and are quite stable, but the dunes close to shore are constantly changing due to wind and movement of soil.

Indiana

The Growth of Indiana

In today's Indiana you'll find an international seaport on the Lake Michigan shoreline, towboats pushing barges of coal and corn down the Ohio River, and a web of roads and railroads. But about eight thousand years ago, Indiana was a land of Native Americans. Hundreds of their mounds and artifacts are found throughout the state. For instance, at Sonotabac Mounds, near Vincennes, the Woodlands people left behind pieces of pottery and stone tools. At Angel Mounds National Park, near Evansville along the Ohio River, Mississippian people built a mound community that covers 430 acres of land. The largest mound is 44 feet high and covers four acres of land. These Native Americans grew vegetables and tobacco. They wove cloth and fished in the rivers with intricate nets. They buried their dead with care and ceremony.

By the time French explorers arrived, around 1650, the Mississippian Native Americans were gone. The land was occupied by the Miami, Delaware, Mohegan, Shawnee, and Huron. Some of these groups

Tecumseh united several Native American groups in an attempt to keep their land.

had been pushed west from the area that is now Ohio by the Iroquois. The Iroquois themselves were being pushed west by European settlers. Other groups had moved south from what is now Michigan. These Native American groups hunted and trapped in a land of thick forests and clear lakes.

The French explorers weren't looking for land. They were looking for people to convert to the Catholic faith and to trade with for furs. The French already had a settlement at Detroit, in the Michigan region, and they were exploring widely, especially on the Great Lakes and the Mississippi River. They wanted a short cut from Detroit to the Mississippi. So they paddled and carried their canoes to the Wabash River, near what is now Fort Wayne. The Wabash winds down along the region at an angle. Finally it washes into the Ohio River, and the Ohio flows into the Mississippi. It was a perfect trade route.

To protect this trade route, the French built three forts on the Wabash in the area of present-day Fort Wayne, Lafayette, and Vincennes. Troops were stationed at the forts to protect the traders. In 1732 the French built a settlement in Vincennes. This was the first European settlement in the Indiana region.

Soon both French and British trappers and traders were moving through the area. The British and the French were rivals for the fur trade, however. They both wanted all the land between the Allegheny Mountains and the Mississippi River. In 1756 the rivalry finally erupted in the French and Indian War. It was called that because most Native Americans

Robert Cavelier, Sieur de La Salle, was the first European to visit present-day Indiana. He was looking for a water route to the Pacific Ocean.

supported and helped the French at that time. Very little fighting took place in the Indiana region during the war. When the fighting finally ended in 1763, Britain had gained control of all of the land east of the Mississippi River. Indiana became part of what was called the Northwest Territory.

That same year, Pontiac, an Ottawa leader, organized thousands of Native Americans in an effort to drive out the British. Pontiac's followers defeated the British troops at Fort Wayne and Lafayette. After a long siege, Pontiac failed to capture Detroit. The Native Americans withdrew, and the fighting stopped.

In 1777, during the Revolutionary War, British troops were sent to Vincennes to protect the area against the American forces. George Rogers Clark and a number of French and American volunteers attacked the fort at Vincennes. For two years, ownership of the fort switched hands. Finally, in 1779 Clark took control of the area.

Before the Revolutionary War ended in 1783, only a few hardy traders and settlers had crossed the Appalachians into the old Northwest Territory. After 1790 a flood of

George Rogers Clark took control of the Vincennes area from the British during the Revolutionary War.

The Tippecanoe Ancient Fife and Drum Corps—named in honor of the battle at Tippecanoe Creek—leads a military unit that is on parade.

Old farmsteads can be found in the heart of Indiana farmland.

people rushed west to stake out farms on the rich soil. In 1800 a territorial government was set up and the region became part of the Indiana Territory. This area included present-day Indiana and Wisconsin, and parts of Michigan and Minnesota. As settlers moved in, clashes with the Native Americans increased. Under leaders such as the Miami chief known as Little Turtle, Native Americans won many battles.

But ultimately the Native Americans began losing the wars. Every time they lost, they signed a treaty that gave more of their land to the settlers. Then, Shawnee chief Tecumseh and his brother Tenskwatawa (known as the Prophet) tried to persuade Native Americans living in the Indiana Territory to hold on to their land.

Their plan was to unite all Native American groups in a confederation against the Americans. The brothers would meet with their followers in the village known as Prophet's Town at the junction of the Wabash River and Tippecanoe Creek.

In 1811 William Henry Harrison, governor of Indiana Territory, went to Prophet's Town. Tecumseh was in the south, meeting with other Native American groups about the confederation. The Prophet and his followers attacked Harrison and his troops. Harrison defeated the Native Americans at the Battle of Tippecanoe. As a result of the battle, Tecumseh's confederation was destroyed in Indiana. Harrison later used his victory at Tippecanoe to help him win election as the ninth President of the United States.

In 1816 Indiana became the nineteenth state of the United States. Its constitution was like those of other states, except for two special provisions: the state prohibited slavery, and it called for the establishment of a public school system. Indiana was the first state to decree that everyone should be educated.

The United States government felt more settlers would come into the area if the Native Americans did not live there. As a result, the government decided to remove the Native Americans to the West. One group of Native Americans after another was removed from the state. The Potawatomi were forced out of central Indiana into Kansas in 1837. So many people died on the way that the trail they followed has been called the "Trail of Death." By 1846 most of the Miami also had been transferred to the West.

The first Indiana railroad, established in 1834, consisted of a horse pulling a car over the tracks at Shelbyville. By 1860, Indiana had 2,200 miles of railroad track. Today, more railroad traffic passes through Indiana than almost any other state.

The northern part of the state remained unsettled for a long time. The land there was sandy and swampy, so it was hard to farm. The land in southern Indiana was much better for this purpose. Also, the southern portion had forests, which the settlers needed for lumber to build settlements. Until about 1830, there were few roads to travel on, so most settlers from the East came by boat, usually down the Ohio River. It was easier to settle the central part of the state after the federal government built the National Road from east to west, through Indianapolis to Terre Haute. When the National Road was finished, it went all the way from the state of Maryland to St. Louis, Missouri. About the same time, the north-south Michigan Road was built from Detroit to the Ohio River, passing through Indianapolis.

The state did its part by building trails and roads between towns. In 1834 the first railroad arrived in Shelbyville, outside of Indianapolis. By the 1850s rail systems also were built throughout the central and southern regions. Within another ten years the state had 2,200 miles of railroad tracks. These roads and railways were crucial, not just for the citizens of the state, but for the westward movement of American settlers.

Before the Civil War, the Underground Railroad was active throughout the state. This wasn't a real railroad. It was a system of people—families and

The home of Levi Coffin, left, and Catherine Coffin, right, was called "the Grand Central Station of the Underground Railroad."

individuals—who secretly helped runaway slaves travel from the slave states to freedom in the North. There were three main routes through Indiana. One Quaker couple, Levi and Catherine Coffin, lived in Fountain City, which is near the Indiana-Ohio border. The Coffins helped more than two thousand slaves escape.

When the Civil War began in 1861, Indiana's railroads proved to be important for the Union. The railways were used to quickly transfer soldiers and goods closer to the South. More than two hundred thousand Indiana soldiers fought in the Union Army. But, because many settlers in the state had come from Southern states, the Confederacy claimed some supporters as well.

There was no Civil War fighting in Indiana until 1863. Confederate General John Hunt Morgan led a group of soldiers—known as Morgan's Raiders— across the Ohio River from Kentucky. Morgan raided

John Hunt Morgan and his raiders were known for attacking quickly and retreating. They burned bridges, stole horses, and captured Union supplies.

Corydon, which had been the first capital of the state. He and his raiders were forced back.

The years after the Civil War were hard. Indiana was very poor. There was very little money to generate statewide projects to develop the state's resources. Most of the farms produced only enough food to support the local community. Finally, in the 1890s, Indiana farmers began growing wheat. There was a great demand for that crop in the East where most of the United States population lived. The money from the sale of wheat brought changes for the better in Indiana.

In 1889 the Standard Oil Company built one of the world's largest oil refineries in Whiting, along the shore of Lake Michigan at the north end of Indiana. Inland Steel was started in Chicago Heights, Indiana, in 1893. In 1906 the United States Steel Corporation built an entire city to house the workers for its new steel mill. The city was named Gary. U.S. Steel built homes for one hundred thousand families. By 1920 Gary was the sixth largest city in the state. More than half of its citizens had been born in Europe.

Iron ore was brought to the steel mills by way of Lake Michigan. Railroads brought coal from southern Indiana to fire the blast furnaces. Finished steel was shipped out by the same methods.

Industries didn't come without hardships. Conditions were very harsh for people working in the mills, refineries, and other

This is the Amoco refinery in Whiting. When Standard Oil built the first refinery in Whiting, it was the largest in the world.

businesses. Men, women, and children worked long hours, and the conditions were dangerous.

The automobile industry also became an important part of the Indiana economy. In 1894 Elwood Haynes of Kokomo built one of the first gasoline-powered automobiles. Haynes was the first person to break the seven-miles-an-hour speed record!

This man is making horse harnesses in the Studebaker factory.

The Studebaker brothers of South Bend had opened a wagon shop before the Civil War. The Studebaker Company supplied wagons to the Union during the war, and later the company built prairie schooners for people moving west. By 1902 Studebaker was building electric cars and trucks. In 1914 the cars had gasoline engines. The company continued to produce cars until the 1960s.

Other early automobile manufacturers were also located in Indiana—companies like Auburn, Stutz, Dusenberg, and Marmon. About 1909 automobile manufacturers built a dirt track in Indianapolis to test their new models. The purpose of the track changed in 1911. That's when the first 500-mile Memorial Day automobile race—the Indy 500—was run.

In the 1920s European immigrants and African Americans from the South flooded into the northern region of Indiana. They were lured by the possibility of

On the Fourth of July, 1894, Elwood Haynes tested out his new car. The car's top speed was seven miles per hour.

employment in the steel mills and oil refineries. The Ku Klux Klan was an organization of people who were opposed to the influx of European immigrants and African Americans. The KKK had more than 250,000 members across the state, and they harassed and terrorized these new workers, particularly the African Americans. The organization lost its influence in the later part of the 1920s.

Things were changing in Indiana. By the end of World War I, more people worked in industries than in agriculture. These people found themselves out of work in the 1930s when the Great Depression gripped the nation. Like other states, Indiana didn't begin an economic recovery until the United States became involved in World War II. Thousands of people went back to work in factories, producing war materials.

After the war, shipbuilding and steel industries flourished. Standard Oil continued to build refineries along the Lake Michigan shore. By the 1960s Indiana was ranked as the best place in the country for new businesses. The state could point to extensive rail transportation, good interstate roads, and shipping on the lake and on the Ohio River.

The 1960s saw the beginning of another economic trend. Middle-class families could afford to move out of urban areas and into the suburbs. The cities lost much of their revenue because the families that remained were usually those who couldn't afford to leave. But the cities still had to provide services—things like schools, hospitals, police officers, and fire departments. In many cases, movement out of the cities was along racial lines, because many African Americans still did not have enough income to move. The change could be seen in politics. In Gary in 1967, Richard G. Hatcher was the first African American to be elected mayor of a major American city.

It wasn't until after the Civil War that the Ohio River was considered a major waterway for commercial traffic. Today, the Ohio River carries more commercial traffic than any other river in the United States, except for the Mississippi.

In the 1970s Indiana constructed a port for ocean-going vessels. These ships carry cargo to and from Great Lakes ports by going through the St. Lawrence Seaway. But the steel and automobile industries were hit by hard times in the late 1970s and the 1980s. There were agricultural problems as well. Many families had to sell their farms and look for jobs in the cities. To meet rising costs, the state was forced to institute a sales tax. All through the 1990s, Indiana has had to deal with the same problems.

The state's traditional base has been in agriculture. When people had to leave the farms, they often had to perform jobs for which they had no skill. Changes like these force people to find different ways of doing things. Sometimes these new ways are better, too. Today, there is positive growth in the state. Much of it is due to the hard work, steadfastness, and adaptability of the citizens of Indiana.

A Utopian Village

Do you believe that such a thing as a perfect society is possible? Robert Owen believed it. In 1824 he bought the town of New Harmony, Indiana, on the banks of the Wabash River. His goal was to form a society in which all members of a community would work together. Each person would do an equal share of the work and receive an equal share of the profits. In this way all community members would actually own the community together. Owen felt that this type of enlightened community, or utopia, could only be possible through education. To accomplish his goal he gathered together scholars, scientists, and educators. In 1825 Owen's hand-picked community arrived in New Harmony by boat.

Robert Owen's son, geologist David Dale Owen, lived in this house in New Harmony. Owen conducted geological surveys of five states while he lived here. Now the house is a museum full of exhibits on David Owen's life and work.

These passengers became known as the "boatload of knowledge." Others yearning to live in such a society soon followed. New Harmony quickly became known as the intellectual heart of the pioneer West.

New Harmony had a lot going for it. The only thing it didn't have was a way for its residents to support themselves. The town had no factories and no industry. The people did not have farming skills. Because they neither made anything they could sell nor grew their own food, they had to buy whatever they needed. That proved to be a very expensive way to live because they had no way to earn the income to pay for things! In 1827 the utopian community failed. The town itself was never abandoned, however. Gradually it came to resemble any other Indiana town.

In the 1940s, Jane Owen visted New Harmony. She was the wife of one of Robert Owen's descendants. She began a project to restore the town and preserve its history. Today, visitors to New Harmony can see the fruits of Ms. Owen's efforts. The village looks much the same as it did in the 1800s. Museums and

Robert Owen's idea for achieving the perfect society included providing a well-rounded education for everyone in the community.

historic homes are open to the public. Another reminder of the New Harmony community that still exists is the Labyrinth. This is a maze of hedges—a three-dimensional puzzle full of twists and turns and dead ends. Those savvy—or lucky—enough to reach the end of the Labyrinth find a temple that the New Harmony community erected there. New Harmony is a town that Robert Owen wanted to live in. Although the town failed, he had set out to make his dream a reality. So, for several years, Robert Owen lived in his idea of a utopia.

Production and Progress

In terms of area, Indiana is the smallest state west of the Appalachian Mountains, except for Hawaii. In fact, it's only the thirty-eighth largest state in the United States, and it's the smallest state in the Midwest. But there are other ways to decide how "big" a state is.

If you measure size in terms of population, Indiana is the fourteenth largest state in the country. If you measure size in terms of economy, it is the tenth leading state in farming and the eleventh leading state in manufacturing. So, there's more to Indiana than its geographical size tells you.

To get a really clear view of what makes Indiana work, take a look at its gross state product. That is the amount of money produced by the various businesses in the state. You have to look at services first because that part of the economy brings in the most money in the state. Service industries are those in which people don't manufacture an actual product. Instead, they may work at a department store, bank, or insurance company. These businesses bring in almost two thirds of the

This blast furnace belongs to U.S. Steel Corporation. Indiana produces more raw steel than any other state, making more than twenty percent of all the steel made in the United States.

state's gross state product. Indiana's most important service industries are retail trade and wholesale trade. Retail businesses sell things to customers, and whole-sale businesses supply the goods to sell to customers.

Manufacturing accounts for about 28 percent of Indiana's gross state product. Manufacturing plays such a large part in the state's economy because of Indiana's extensive railroad and highway systems. When raw materials or finished goods are shipped from the East to the West or vice versa, many of them move on transportation routes through Indiana. The state has 11,300 miles of state and interstate highways. It has three major ports. One is Burns Harbor on Lake Michigan, and two are on the Ohio River, in Madison and in Evansville. Indiana has smaller ports, too, in places such as Whiting and Hammond. Indiana railroads handle more freight traffic than almost any other state. Indiana's airports also handle freight.

What kinds of things are manufactured in Indiana? Indiana produces more steel than any other state in the country—about 23 million tons of raw steel a year. The steel industry was in economic trouble in the 1980s because of competition from foreign manufacturers. But Indiana has responded well. For instance, Inland Steel now produces specialty steel structures with Nissan, a Japanese automobile manufacturer. Some other Indiana companies have turned to processing aluminum.

Although the Studebaker Company no longer makes automobiles in Indiana,

Indiana's largest port, Burns Harbor, provides manufacturers with access to the St. Lawrence Seaway. From there ships can reach ports all over the world. Indiana has a total of three ports, which handle six million tons of cargo every year.

car manufacturing isn't dead. In fact, Indiana is the leading manufacturer of four-wheel drive recreational vehicles, or RVs. Over forty percent of these domestic models are made in Indiana. In addition, a large number of companies produce parts for cars, trucks, and other types of transportation.

Indiana's businesses manufacture other things as well. Elkhart calls itself the "Instrument Capital of the Nation," because a number of its companies produce brass and reed musical instruments. Pharmaceutical companies, such as Eli Lilly, produce medicines and other health and personal care products. Many Indiana companies are branching out into high-tech industries in electrical switching and relay devices, scientific instruments, environmental control instruments, and radio and television receivers.

Agriculture accounts for three percent of the state gross product, so farming isn't as important in Indiana as it used to be. Until World War I, Indiana remained primarily a farming state. In 1920 just over half of Indiana's population lived in its cities. By 1980, almost two thirds had moved into urban areas. But, even though manufacturing has moved ahead of agriculture, farming is still important.

Indiana is ideal for raising most grain crops. The state has rich and fertile soil. It has plenty of water in hundreds of natural lakes. It also averages enough rain every year to grow crops. And its people, from the very beginning, have worked hard to make agriculture possible in Indiana. Originally most of the state was covered with forests. People cut down thousands of

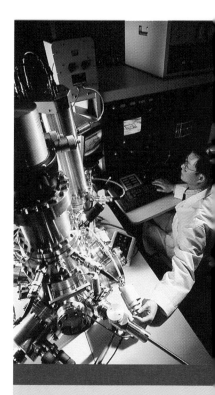

This technician is operating an Auger electron scanner at Delco Electronics.

Indiana's flat fields are rich and fertile. The silos on the right hold much of this farm's harvested corn.

acres of trees in the northern part of the state to clear the land for farming.

Indiana's farms produce corn, soybeans, and grains and grasses, such as wheat and hay. Vegetable farms produce tomatoes, cucumbers, and other truck crops. Most of the orchards produce apples, but there are other crops, too. Indiana farmers also raise hogs and cattle. Milk is a leading farm product in the state. Only California produces more eggs than Indiana.

Minerals are also important to Indiana's economy. One percent of the gross state product comes from mining. About three fourths of that comes from coal. But limestone is also an important product. In fact, almost all of the limestone in the Empire State Building in New York City comes from a quarry near Oolitic in central Indiana. People also mine gravel, sand, and crushed stone in central Indiana. To the south, there are oil fields.

So Indiana has changed over the years. In some ways, it has a long way to go. In the 1980s and 1990s, industries all over the country started modernizing and downsizing. That is another way of saying that the companies decided to produce the same amount of goods and services while employing fewer people. Modern machinery now does much of the work. That trend has affected Indiana's economy because many people have lost their jobs. But the twenty-first century brings the promise of new jobs and new business opportunities. Indiana is aware of that promise and is poised with an energetic and reliable work force.

Until the Civil War, little mining was done in Indiana. Since then, companies have strip-mined for coal, clay, rock, stone, sand, and gravel.

Indiana is a top producer of corn, soybeans, and other field grains.

The Indy

It began as a dirt oval track for testing new automobile designs. The first actual race was held in 1911. The event must have been exciting. Flying car parts and tires endangered the spectators, who kept running out on the track to see what was happening. The police and other guards kept very busy. All in all, no one was bored. The 500-mile race was stopped after 235 miles because the track was falling apart. The track surface was made up of tar and crushed rock. The man who won that race, Ray Harroun, set a record. His average speed was 74.59 miles per hour.

Today, at the Indianapolis 500—or the Indy—some things are the same. The race is still a blur of high octane and high spirits. But the rest of the scene is very different. Long, low cars streak past on the oval track. The streamlined race cars can reach speeds of two hundred miles an hour. Spectators sit in high bleachers all around the oval track and cheer the drivers on. The Indy has become the largest single-day sporting event in the world. More than three hundred thousand people attend the race every year. It is the crowning event of a whole week of celebration.

Only 33 cars can take part in the race. Because of the size of the track, the cars are arranged in rows of three.

Race cars streak down the straightaway of the Indianapolis 500's oval track.

Indy champion Al Unser, Jr., makes a pit stop for refueling. Pit crew members usually include car mechanics, designers, builders, timekeepers, and car owners.

Many more than 33 drivers want to participate in the race, however. All of them want to have a position close to the starting line. So, during the week before the race, Indy officials hold time trials. At the trials, individual drivers, one at a time, race their cars around the track several times. Officials record the speed of each driver. The person with the fastest speed is given the best position, the person with the second fastest speed gets the second best position, and so on.

The cars that run at the Indy are built just for this race. They're called Formula 1 racing cars. The body of the car is very light. The engine is situated just behind the driver. It can produce more than 700 horsepower. By comparison, a standard luxury car produces about 350 horsepower. The gasoline is a special mixture that would not work in the engine of a normal car. An Indy car's gas tank is specially constructed. It is filled with a sponge-like material so that if a crash occurs, the gasoline doesn't splash and cause terrible fires.

Many people don't realize that there's a serious side to the Indy. Safety

The first Indy champion, Ray Harroun, appears here in the winning car, the Marmon Wasp. If he looks tired, it's because he'd been racing for 6 hours, 42 minutes, and 8 seconds.

is important for the drivers. Today, we take it for granted that drivers wear helmets. But the first Indy driver to wear a helmet was Wilbur Shaw, after he had a crash in 1923 and fractured his skull. Even so, other drivers made fun of Shaw for wearing a helmet. Then Shaw had another crash. He was thrown from his car and skidded on his head, but he survived. Today, every driver wears a special helmet. The helmet's special face plate has five

layers. If oil or dirt splatter on the face plate and make it hard to see, the driver just lifts up the dirty layer. The next layer, clear and clean, is ready.

Most people who go to the race don't think about safety concerns. They talk about the cars waiting at the starting line for the command "Drivers, start your engines!" The powerful roar of those 33 engines almost drowns out the cheering. A car called the "pace car" starts down the straight-away, pacing the race cars arranged in their rows of three. The pace car begins to pick up speed. The racers have to keep up, which is no problem, and stay in position, which *can* be a problem. Then, close to the starting line, the pace car pulls out of the way. The starter waves a green flag, and the drivers step on the gas. This time the roar does drown out all other sounds. The race is on!

Indy drivers stop for adjustments to their cars in areas called pits. A pit crew can refuel and repair a car in seconds. They have to be fast—even the slightest delay could lose the race for a driver.

The Indy is a family tradition for some racers. Michael Andretti is the son of Mario Andretti, the only driver ever to win the Grand Prix, the Daytona 500, and the Indy. In 1994 Al Unser, Jr., son of retired four-time Indy champion Al Unser, drank the traditional milk in the Winner's Circle. Indy winners have drunk milk ever since winner Louis Meyer asked for a bottle of milk in 1928.

Since that first race in 1911, Indiana and the world have celebrated the power and excitement of the automobile in Indianapolis. Given the speed of the cars that whip around the oval track, the safety record is amazing. The automotive technology that has come from the race has increased the safety and efficiency of cars everywhere. And, most importantly, the spectators enjoy it!

When the race is over, the winning driver is brought to the Winner's Circle, which is right behind the pit area. It is traditional to present the driver with a wreath, an enormous trophy, and some ice cold milk.

31

The Land, the Music— and Basketball

Today it's easy to entertain ourselves—we have televisions, VCRs, computers, and CD players. We can go out to a movie or a play or visit a museum. But many years ago, after chores and work were done, people had to entertain themselves and each other. Indiana has continued that tradition.

In those old days, when a circus came to town, it was a special occasion. About a hundred years ago, a circus came to Peru, Indiana. The circus owners needed Benjamin Wallace's livery stable—a place where they could buy hay and have their horses cared for. Mr. Wallace usually got paid just before the circus moved to the next town. One year the circus couldn't pay Mr. Wallace. So, instead of collecting what was owed to him, Mr. Wallace became part owner of the circus. By 1934 the Hagenback/Wallace Circus was one of the biggest in the country. Today, Peru has a circus museum with items from the past and the present. Every summer the townspeople present an amateur circus. It's a way to honor the past and entertain themselves and others.

There's no place like Indiana to play high school basketball. Here, Bryce Drew of Valparaiso, Indiana—Mr. Basketball 1994—tries for two points in the 1994 state finals.

This photo shows an opera production at Indiana University. Singers like these study their art all their lives.

Actor William Shatner chats with Hoosier David Letterman. Letterman, who hosts *The Late Show with David Letterman,* was born in Indianapolis and attended Ball State University in Muncie.

Indiana also produces more formal musical sounds than the melodies of the circus calliope. Walk through the campus of Indiana University, for instance, and you'll hear musicians practicing their art. This top-ranked music school is the biggest in the nation. Every year, people from all over the state come to the university to hear its opera company, orchestras, bands, small musical groups, and solo performers.

Music in Indiana can also be a little more "down home." Summer is the time for country music and bluegrass festivals to be held all over the state. Some people feel that the Bill Monroe Bluegrass Festival held in Beanblossom is one of the best in the country. July is the time for people in Evansville to celebrate the Freedom Festival. This event includes music for almost everyone's taste, not to mention hydroplane races up and down the Ohio River.

Indiana is the home of many different kinds of musicians. Michael Jackson, Janet Jackson, and the rest of their family are from Gary; rocker John Mellencamp lives in Seymour; and Peru claims Cole Porter—a songwriter and composer who is known for his jazz, show tunes, and easy melodies.

Literature is also part of a culture, and some of America's great authors are from Indiana. Terre Haute is the birthplace of Theodore Dreiser, an early twentieth century novelist. He is considered one of America's best. Kurt Vonnegut is another writer who is a native of Indiana. Vonnegut is a nationally recognized satirist—a person who criticizes modern life, but does it in a funny way.

Indiana's cities have plenty of cultural attractions. Indianapolis has its own symphony orchestra, which is considered one of the best in the country. Also in Indianapolis is the Indiana Civic Theater. It is the oldest continuously active theater in the country. The Children's Museum of Indianapolis is the largest children's museum in the world. There you'll find

Traditional folk music is important in Indiana culture.

Many dollmakers, potters, metal craftspeople, weavers, and woodworkers display their wares in Brown County. The main street of Nashville, Indiana, shown here, is lined with craft shops.

The Children's Museum in Indianapolis is the largest children's museum in the world. It contains many cultural, historical, and scientific exhibits.

exhibits about history, science, and different cultures. Nashville, Indiana, outside of Bloomington, is a thoroughly cultural place. In Nashville you'll find painters, sculptors, photographers, and musicians all living and working in one of America's best-known art colonies.

One reason tourists come to Indiana is to enjoy its natural resources. The culture of a place is reflected not only in its love for the arts but also in its respect for the environment. For instance, in the early 1900s, the sand dunes along the Lake Michigan shoreline were in danger of being destroyed. So, in 1926 the state protected 2,182 acres for the Indiana Dunes State Park. But that wasn't enough; the state required federal assistance for the park. In 1966 the national government established the Indiana Dunes National Lakeshore. This park now consists of 14,000 acres of the Lake Michigan shoreline.

Much of northern Indiana is flat. But in southeastern Indiana you'll find sharp hills and gullies, rivers and waterfalls, and bluffs and caves. The land there is almost completely covered with forests. The Hoosier National Forest, in Brown County, preserves this landscape. There you'll find ancient trees, such as a grove of black walnuts that are between 150 and 600 years old. Other unspoiled parks in Indiana, like Turkey Run and the Shades, were established in the early 1900s to preserve Indiana's heritage.

Because Abraham Lincoln spent his childhood in Indiana, the state has erected a National Memorial to him near Lincoln City. The Memorial includes the burial site of Lincoln's mother, Nancy Hanks. There's also a special "Living Historical Farm," which is a restoration of the Lincoln farm, complete with farmhouse, fields, and gardens.

No discussion of Indiana culture would be complete without mentioning sports, especially basketball. Probably no other sport is so representative of Indiana culture as high school basketball. In fact, people in Indiana proudly call the basketball season "Hoosier Hysteria." The fans—thousands of them—are fired up for months. The competition is fierce. All schools compete with each other, no matter how big or how small, and loyalties run deep. Some schools even close during the week of the sectionals, which is the first elimination round for the state championship tournament.

Hoosier is a term that refers to someone from Indiana. Some have traced the word to the term *husher*, meaning "a river boat worker strong enough to hush any challenger." Others claim the word comes from *hoozer*, an Anglo-Saxon word meaning "hill dweller." Although the origin of the term is not known for certain, one thing is sure—that Hoosiers bear their nickname proudly.

Although Abraham Lincoln was born in Kentucky, he grew up in Indiana. Lincoln's family moved to this Indiana farm in 1816, when Lincoln was seven years old.

The Beauty of Columbus

In some ways, Columbus is just a small Indiana town. About thirty-five thousand people live there. They rely on one major company for a living—Cummins Engine Company, the United States' leading maker of diesel engines. Some of the people work at the Cummins factory. Others work for companies that sell services to Cummins—a nearby lunch counter, a delivery service, and supply companies. If the Cummins plant closed, it would affect almost everyone in Columbus.

But Cummins has brought much more to Columbus residents than a steady paycheck. The company president, J. Irwin Miller, believes that a company has other responsibilities to its community. Mr. Miller hired great architects from all over the world to come to Columbus and design buildings for its people. Now, Columbus is known all over the world. In fact, Columbus is ranked fourth in the nation in architectural achievement—right after New York, Chicago, and Los Angeles.

Because of Mr. Miller, Columbus has become a living art museum. Today, people from all over the country visit Columbus. They

The spire of the North Christian Church reaches 192 feet into the air.

know that this town is the only place in the world where they can look at an Eero Saarinen church through a Henry Moore arch in front of an I. M. Pei library.

Maybe the most important thing about Columbus is that these extraordinary buildings aren't just places to be viewed. They are also places that people use, such as churches, schools, and libraries. One church has a spire that reaches 192 feet into the air.

There's a spectacular mall. Inside this mall is a moving sculpture made out of seven tons of scrap metal.

Columbus can be an inspiring place to live. As a teacher in Columbus said, "When I look at our schools now, since all the new architecture has come along . . . I know absolutely that these buildings have got to make a difference in their lives . . . not only in that day's work, but I think they carry that out of the building, too."

Colonel Conn's Magnificent Musical Instrument Factory

In the past one hundred years, more trumpets, drums, flutes, saxophones, and other musical instruments have been made in Elkhart, Indiana, than anywhere else in the world. The person who started it all was musician and inventor Charles Gerard Conn.

Mr. Conn was born in New York in 1844. His family moved to Elkhart when he was seven. His father, a school teacher, taught him to play the violin and the cornet, a trumpetlike instrument. When he was 17, Gerard Conn left home to join the Union Army and fight in the Civil War.

After the war, Colonel Conn couldn't decide on a career right away. So he worked for a while in a grocery store and in a factory. In time he began inventing parts to make sewing machines work better. These inventions and others eventually led him to make parts for musical instruments. By 1876 he was manufacturing musical instruments.

Colonel Conn's band instruments were made of sparkling brass, shining silver, and gleaming gold. Some very special instruments were decorated with beautiful engravings. Others were even ornamented with diamonds, emeralds, and rubies! Conn Company instruments were sold to musicians all over the world. By the 1890s the Conn Company was so successful that it was

Charles Gerard Conn first began making musical instrument parts when a bully gave him a fat lip. Conn made a soft rubber mouthpiece he could use to keep playing the cornet while his lip healed.

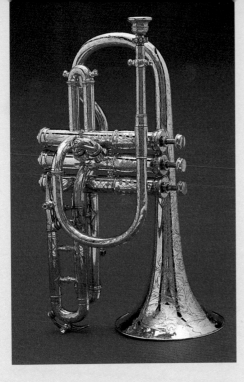

Conn made this jeweled cornet in 1883. A closer look shows that the cornet is covered with elaborate engravings.

This is how the C. G. Conn Musical Instrument Company factory looked in 1910 before the fire. Conn's success in selling musical instruments attracted other instrument makers to Elkhart. By 1940 seventy percent of the wind and percussion instruments made in the United States were being produced there.

advertised as the largest musical instrument factory on earth.

The Conn Company is famous for making several kinds of instruments. For example, the first saxophones made in America were produced by the Conn Company in 1888. The first sousaphones were made at the Conn factory in the 1890s. This instrument, which wraps around the musician's body, is usually the largest horn in the marching band. Colonel Conn also manufactured an instrument that he invented himself. It is a cross between an English horn and a saxophone, which he called the Conn-O-Sax.

In 1910 Conn's factory burned to the ground. A few years after he rebuilt the factory, Colonel Conn sold the factory and retired. The company that bought the factory still makes Conn instruments. Colonel Conn died in 1931. His dreams continue to live on today, however, in the more than one million instruments that bear his name.

Looking Forward

Indiana has faced many tough problems in the past and solved them with creative answers. For instance, in southern Indiana, the usual way to mine coal was to strip mine. Strip mines have deep pits dug out to remove the coal. The pit is dug layer by layer until all the coal is removed. Then the mining companies move on, leaving behind the stripped and bare land. Indiana passed a law demanding that mining companies restore the land when they are done mining. Some of these areas were turned into parks, for example. Creative answers are a tradition in Indiana.

Indiana's steel mills are very old. In the 1980s the steel companies began to lose business to companies in other countries. One reason was that the foreign companies had more modern equipment. Many of Indiana's mills had to close, and many people lost their jobs. Other mills in Indiana, however, bought new equipment. They decided that they couldn't keep making every kind of steel as they had been doing. Instead they would concentrate on just one kind of

Indianapolis is one of the largest cities in the United States. It also has one of the lowest crime rates of any United States city.

Gary is a major industrial area. Growth in major businesses will help ensure a healthy future.

steel or one kind of steel product. Some companies began producing aluminum instead. The ability to change shows that Indiana companies can continue to prosper and provide jobs for Indiana workers.

Indiana is now exploring other new kinds of industries. For example, the state already is one of the leading manufacturers of electronic equipment. Indiana is searching for ways to attract even more new businesses, because that is the way to ensure work for its citizens.

Indiana's biggest challenge in the future may be in helping individuals to change, instead of companies. Many people in rural areas have been moving to the cities. There aren't as many jobs in the farm areas as there once were. Sometimes these people can't find work because they don't have the skills to do the new jobs. One solution to this problem is to help people learn new job skills, such as using computers. There are other possible solutions as well.

So how will Indiana solve its future problems? It will continue to rely on the creativity of its business leaders and its strong tradition of individual effort.

Important Historical Events

1679 The French explorer Robert Cavelier, Sieur de La Salle, crosses Indiana on the St. Joseph and Kankakee rivers.

1704 to 1732 The French build three forts: Fort Miami (at Ft. Wayne), Fort Quiatenon (at Lafayette), and Vincennes.

1763 The French and Indian War ends with a treaty. Indiana is ceded to Great Britain by France.

1779 George Rogers Clark establishes control of Vincennes.

1783 Indiana is included in the area that Great Britain gives to the United States after the Revolutionary War.

1787 Indiana becomes part of the Northwest Territory.

1800 The Indiana Territory is established. Vincennes becomes the capital, and William Henry Harrison is the first territorial governor.

1811 William Henry Harrison defeats Tenskwatawa at the Battle of Tippecanoe.

1813 The capital of the Indiana Territory is moved to Corydon.

1815 George Rapp, leader of the Harmony Society, establishes a communal settlement called Harmonie.

1816 Indiana becomes the nineteenth state on December 11.

1837 The Potawatomi are removed to Kansas.

1851 A new constitution is adopted, which is still in effect.

1863 Confederate General John Morgan and his Morgan's Raiders attack Corydon by crossing the Ohio River.

1889 Standard Oil Company builds a large oil refinery at Whiting.

1894 Elwood Haynes builds an early automobile in Kokomo.

1906 The city of Gary is founded by the United States Steel Corporation.

1911 The first Memorial Day 500-mile automobile race is held at Indianapolis.

1933 The state government is reorganized; the governor receives greater powers.

1956 The Northern Indiana Toll Road is completed.

1962 Congress agrees to let Indiana have its first national park—the Lincoln Boyhood National Memorial.

1963 The Studebaker Corporation ends automobile production.

1965 The Indiana Department of Natural Resources is created to handle problems of soil erosion and water pollution.

1966 The Indiana Sand Dunes National Lakeshore is established.

1967 Richard D. Hatcher is elected mayor of Gary, becoming Indiana's first African American mayor.

1988 State voters approve a state lottery.

1993 State voters approve riverboat gambling casinos.

The Indiana state flag has a torch surrounded by stars on a field of blue. The torch symbolizes freedom and learning. The 19 stars represent states. Indiana was the 19th state to join the Union.

Indiana Almanac

Nickname. The Hoosier State

Capital. Indianapolis

State Bird. Cardinal

State Flower. Peony

State Tree. Tulip tree

State Motto. The Crossroads of America

State Song. "On the Banks of the Wabash"

State Abbreviations. Ind. (traditional); IN (postal)

Statehood. December 11, 1816, the 19th state

Government. Congress: U.S. senators, 2; U.S. representatives, 10. State Legislature: senators, 50; representatives, 100. Counties: 92

Area. 36,185 sq mi (93,720 sq km), 38th among the states

Greatest Distances. north/south, 273 mi (440 km); east/west, 177 mi (285 km). Shoreline: 45 mi (72 km), on Lake Michigan

Elevation. Highest: Wayne County, 1,257 ft (383 m). Lowest: Ohio River, 320 ft (98 m)

Population. 1990 Census: 5,564,228 (1% increase over 1980), 14th among the states. Density: 154 persons per sq mi (59 persons per sq km). Distribution: 65% urban, 35% rural. 1980 Census: 5,490,224

Economy. *Agriculture:* hogs, cattle, corn, soybeans. *Manufacturing:* primary metals, transportation equipment, electrical machinery, food products. *Mining:* coal, stone

State Seal

State Flower: Peony

State Bird: Cardinal

Annual Events

★ Parke County Maple Fair in Rockville (February)

★ Indiana High School basketball tournament (March)

★ Indianapolis 500-mile Memorial Day Automobile Race

★ Bluegrass Music Festival in Beanblossom (June)

★ Circus Day Festival in Peru (July)

★ Indiana State Fair in Indianapolis (August)

★ Parke County Covered Bridge Festival in Rockville (October)

★ Hydroplane Regatta in Madison (July)

★ National Muzzle-Loading Rifle Association Championship Shoot in Friendship

Places to Visit

★ Amish Acres in Nappannee

★ Angel Mounds, near Evansville

★ Brown County Art Galleries in Nashville

★ Conner Prairie Pioneer Settlement in Nobelsville

★ Eiteljorg Museum of American Indians and Western Art in Indianapolis

★ George Rogers Clark Memorial in Vincennes

★ Indiana Dunes State Park, near Gary

★ Lincoln Boyhood National Memorial, near Lincoln City

★ Sugar Creek covered bridges in Parke County

★ Wyandotte Cave, near Levenworth

Index